WNBA SUPERSTARS

# ELENA DELLE DONNE

by Erin Nicks

FOCUS READERS
NAVIGATOR

## WWW.FOCUSREADERS.COM



Focus Readers is distributed by North Star Editions:
sales@northstareditions.com | 888-417-0195

Produced for Focus Readers by Red Line Editorial.

Photographs ©: Nick Wass/AP Images, cover, 1; G Fiume/Getty Images Sport/Getty Images, 4–5; Rob Carr/Getty Images Sport/Getty Images, 7, 9, 25; Jonathan Daniel/Getty Images Sport/Getty Images, 10–11; G Fiume/Maryland Terrapins/Getty Images Sport/Getty Images, 13; Al Tielemans/Sports Illustrated/Getty Images, 15; Anthony Nesmith/Cal Sport Media/AP Images, 16–17; John Bazemore/AP Images, 19; Danny Moloshok/AP Images, 21; Leon Bennett/Getty Images Sport/Getty Images, 22–23; Jevone Moore/Icon Sportswire/Getty Images, 27; Scott Taetsch/Getty Images Sport/Getty Images, 28

**Library of Congress Cataloging-in-Publication Data**
Library of Congress Cataloging-in-Publication Data is available on the Library of Congress website.

**ISBN**
978-1-63739-066-5 (hardcover)
978-1-63739-120-4 (paperback)
978-1-63739-222-5 (ebook pdf)
978-1-63739-174-7 (hosted ebook)

Printed in the United States of America
Mankato, MN
012022

## ABOUT THE AUTHOR

Erin Nicks has been a professional writer for more than 20 years. She has written for newspapers and websites including NHL.com and Yahoo! Sports, and she is the author of more than 20 books. She is originally from Thunder Bay, Ontario, Canada, and currently resides in Ottawa, Ontario, Canada.

# TABLE OF CONTENTS


CHAPTER 1

From Grit to Glory 5

CHAPTER 2

Standing Tall 11

CHAPTER 3

Reaching for the Sky 17

PAVING THE WAY

Lisa Leslie 21

CHAPTER 4

Moving to the Mystics 23

At a Glance • 29
Focus on Elena Delle Donne • 30
Glossary • 31
To Learn More • 32
Index • 32

SPALDING
25
THOMAS

CHAPTER 1

# FROM GRIT TO GLORY

Elena Delle Donne was in pain. She was playing in the 2019 Women's National Basketball Association (WNBA) Finals. Delle Donne's team, the Washington Mystics, needed her. But she was struggling with a bad back injury. Her spine felt like a metal pole. She had a hard time moving. As a result,

**Elena Delle Donne shoots during Game 5 of the 2019 WNBA Finals between the Washington Mystics and the Connecticut Sun.**

Delle Donne had to limit the number of minutes she played.

The Mystics had made it to the Finals a year earlier. But they got swept by the Seattle Storm three games to none. In 2019, the Mystics had another shot at glory. This time, they were facing the Connecticut Sun. Going into Game 5, the series was tied at two. The winner of Game 5 would win the title. At halftime, the Mystics trailed the Sun 43–42.

The Sun started off strong in the second half. Soon, the Mystics fell behind by nine points. But Delle Donne was hungry. She wasn't going to let injuries get in the way. Plus, the home crowd was

Delle Donne drives toward the basket during Game 5 of the 2019 WNBA Finals.

cheering her on. She hit a layup, and the Washington fans roared. The Mystics pressed on. By the end of the third quarter, they were down by only two. It was all going to come down to the final quarter.

Mystics guard Natasha Cloud sank several baskets early in the fourth. Then Delle Donne and center Emma Meesseman each hit jump shots. Delle Donne didn't let up. When she wasn't scoring, she was pushing past her opponents. She used her body to make room for her teammates. She drove and spun to the net. She drained her free throws. She showed why she was the league's Most Valuable Player (MVP).

The Mystics pulled ahead. With only 2:41 left in the game, the Mystics led 80–72. Delle Donne even nabbed the final rebound before the buzzer sounded. The wild Washington fans leaped to their feet.

Delle Donne celebrates with Mystics teammate Kristi Toliver after winning the 2019 WNBA Finals.

The Mystics had won the championship. Delle Donne beamed with joy as she lifted the silver trophy.

McDONALD'S
ALL AMERICAN
30
McDONALD'S
ALL AMERICAN
11

CHAPTER 2

# STANDING TALL

Elena Delle Donne was born on September 5, 1989. She grew up in Wilmington, Delaware. Elena was always tall for her age. When she was three, a stranger once told Elena's mom that Elena was too old to be using a pacifier. The person had guessed that Elena was eight years old.

**Elena Delle Donne handles the ball during the All American high school girls' game in 2008.**

As she grew, Elena liked to play basketball with her older brother, Gene. In high school, she played basketball at Ursuline Academy. That's when her free-throw game took off. She hit a record-setting 80 free throws in a row during her second year. Elena also developed a great jump shot. Those skills helped her lead the team to three straight state championships.

Elena had started getting college offers when she was only 13. By the time she finished high school, she had many colleges to choose from. In 2008, she decided to attend the University of Connecticut. She went to the school

Delle Donne of the University of Delaware wrestles for the ball during a 2011 game.

but left two days later. She was tired of basketball and missed her family.

Delle Donne moved back to her home state of Delaware. She joined the University of Delaware's volleyball team. She enjoyed playing volleyball. But she missed the speed and defense of basketball. Over time, she began shooting hoops again.

In 2009, Delle Donne was ready to return to basketball. She joined the Delaware Blue Hens as a **redshirt**. She excelled during her four years with the team. She set 45 school records. And

## LOVE FOR LIZZIE

Elena is very close with her older sister, Lizzie. Lizzie has **cerebral palsy** and is autistic. She was also born blind and deaf. Moving back to Delaware allowed Elena to see Lizzie more often. Elena has said that Lizzie is her biggest inspiration. Elena has Lizzie's name tattooed on her side. It is her way of keeping her sister close during games.

Delle Donne dribbles downcourt during a 2012 game with the Delaware Blue Hens.

she scored 3,039 points. She became the No. 5 all-time leading scorer in National Collegiate Athletic Association (NCAA) history. Delle Donne had left basketball and come back. But by 2013, her future in the sport was looking surer than ever.

adidas
SKY
11
SKY
10

CHAPTER 3

# REACHING FOR THE SKY

Elena Delle Donne's WNBA career began in 2013. She was **drafted** second overall by the Chicago Sky. In her first game, she made 22 points and eight rebounds. It was the third-best point total in WNBA history for a first game.

When it was time for the All-Star Game, Delle Donne led the league in voting.

**In 2013, Elena Delle Donne drained 97 free throws. That was a Chicago Sky record for a rookie.**

It was the first time a **rookie** had received the most votes. Delle Donne's size and strength helped her defend against opponents. She finished the season with 54 blocks. That was a Sky record. After her amazing season, Delle Donne was named Rookie of the Year.

The next year was hard for Delle Donne. She'd had Lyme disease since 2008. This disease often causes fevers and tiredness. Over time, it can affect joints and the heart, too. Delle Donne's Lyme disease got worse in 2014. She missed much of the season as a result.

Even so, Delle Donne wasn't going to miss the playoffs. She had a huge

Delle Donne hits a game-winning shot with seconds left in a 2014 playoff game against the Atlanta Dream.

game against the Atlanta Dream. The Sky were down 20 points heading into the fourth quarter. Delle Donne scored 17 points in the fourth. It was the biggest fourth-quarter comeback in the league's history. However, the Sky lost in the Finals to the Phoenix Mercury.

In 2015, Delle Donne won her first MVP award. She led the league in scoring. She averaged 23.4 points and 8.4 rebounds per game. Delle Donne continued to lead the Sky in 2016. But she got injured late in the season. She had to miss the playoffs.

## UNIFIED SPORTS

In 2014, Delle Donne began a new role. She became a Special Olympics global **ambassador**. In this role, she led basketball camps for Special Olympics athletes. Delle Donne also used the role to support unified sports. In unified sports, people with and without intellectual disabilities play together. All of Delle Donne's **clinics** and camps were unified. These efforts built bonds across differences.

# LISA LESLIE

Elena Delle Donne's 2015 MVP season put her in elite company. Basketball experts began comparing her to WNBA legends such as Lisa Leslie. Leslie played 12 seasons in the WNBA. She led the Los Angeles Sparks to two championships. In 2001, Leslie became the first player to win the regular season MVP, All-Star Game MVP, and Finals MVP in the same season. In 2002, she became the first WNBA player to dunk in league history. In 2011, fans voted Leslie one of the top 15 all-time WNBA players.

Lisa Leslie of the Los Angeles Sparks drives to the basket during a 2006 WNBA game.

SPALDING
3
PARKER
mystics
11
SPALDING

CHAPTER 4

# MOVING TO THE MYSTICS

Elena Delle Donne was traded before the 2017 season. She went from the Chicago Sky to the Washington Mystics. The Mystics were thrilled to have Delle Donne on their team. Delle Donne could score, rebound, and block shots. And the Mystics had struggled for many years. In fact, the team had gone 19 seasons

**Elena Delle Donne blocks a shot from Candace Parker of the Los Angeles Sparks during a 2017 game with the Mystics.**

without making the Finals. Washington fans hoped Delle Donne could turn things around.

Delle Donne did just that. In 2017, she had her best free-throw percentage to date, with .953. She did the same with her field-goal percentage, with .494. The Mystics advanced to the **Conference** finals for the first time since 2002.

Delle Donne brought the team to new heights in 2018. She led the Mystics in points, rebounds, and blocked shots. And by July 2018, she had become the fastest WNBA player to score 3,000 points. She reached the goal in only 148 games. She led the Mystics to their first-ever

Delle Donne drives past Natasha Howard of the Seattle Storm during Game 3 of the 2018 WNBA Finals.

Finals. They didn't win, but 2019 was just around the corner.

Many basketball experts said Delle Donne was the best free-throw shooter in the game. Her career free-throw percentage was the highest in the WNBA.

It was also higher than any National Basketball Association (NBA) player's free-throw percentage. One key to Delle Donne's free-throw success was keeping things simple. She moved as little of her body as possible.

Delle Donne did not make many mistakes in 2019. In fact, she became the first WNBA player to join the 50-40-90 club. That season, she shot more than 50 percent from the field. She hit above 40 percent from three-point range. And she was well above 90 percent at the line. By the end of 2020, only eight NBA players had reached the 50-40-90 mark. Delle Donne's talent

Delle Donne shoots a jumper during a 2019 game against the Sparks.

helped make the Mystics champions for the first time ever.

Delle Donne's time at the top took a pause in 2020. The COVID-19 **pandemic** spread around the world that year. Having **chronic** Lyme disease put Delle Donne

Delle Donne attempts a layup during a 2019 playoff game against the Las Vegas Aces.

at greater risk of becoming seriously ill from the virus. So, she chose not to play in the 2020 season. Even so, she had proved time and again to be one of the WNBA's best players. And Mystics fans hoped she would lead the team to more championships.

# ELENA DELLE DONNE

- Height: 6 feet 5 inches (196 cm)
- Weight: 187 pounds (85 kg)
- Birth date: September 5, 1989
- Birthplace: Wilmington, Delaware
- High school: Ursuline Academy (Wilmington, Delaware)
- College: University of Delaware (Newark, Delaware) (2009–2013)
- Pro teams: Chicago Sky (2013–2016); Washington Mystics (2017–)
- Major awards: WNBA Rookie of the Year (2013); WNBA All-Star (2013–2015, 2017–2019); WNBA MVP (2015, 2019); WNBA champion (2019)

## FOCUS ON

# ELENA DELLE DONNE

*Write your answers on a separate piece of paper.*

1. Write a letter to a friend describing what you learned about Elena Delle Donne's first season in the WNBA.
2. At one point, Delle Donne got tired of playing basketball. Could you ever get sick of playing a sport? Which one, and why?
3. Going into the 2021 season, Delle Donne had the highest career percentage of what kind of shot?
   - **A.** field goal
   - **B.** free throw
   - **C.** three point
4. Why does moving as little of her body as possible help Delle Donne make free throws?
   - **A.** With less motion, Delle Donne can use more strength.
   - **B.** With less motion, Delle Donne can shoot much farther.
   - **C.** With less motion, there are fewer chances for mistakes.

*Answer key on page 32.*

# GLOSSARY

**ambassador**
An official representative of a country or organization.

**cerebral palsy**
A condition caused by brain damage around the time of birth, often leading to speech and muscle disabilities.

**chronic**
Impacting someone for a long period of time.

**clinics**
Events that teach a skill in an activity.

**conference**
A group of teams within a league.

**drafted**
Selected in a draft. A draft is a system that allows teams to acquire new players coming into a league.

**pandemic**
A disease that spreads quickly around the world.

**redshirt**
A member of a college team who can practice with the team but can't play in games.

**rookie**
A professional athlete in his or her first year.

# TO LEARN MORE

## BOOKS

Hoehn, Jim. *WNBA*. Minneapolis: Abdo Publishing, 2021.

Kelley, K. C. *WNBA Records and Trivia*. Mankato, MN: The Child's World, 2020.

Omoth, Tyler. *The WNBA Finals*. North Mankato, MN: Capstone Press, 2020.

## NOTE TO EDUCATORS

Visit **www.focusreaders.com** to find lesson plans, activities, links, and other resources related to this title.

# INDEX

All-Star Game, 17, 21
Atlanta Dream, 19

Chicago Sky, 17–20, 23
Cloud, Natasha, 8
Connecticut Sun, 6
COVID-19 pandemic, 27

Delle Donne, Lizzie, 14

Leslie, Lisa, 21
Los Angeles Sparks, 21
Lyme disease, 18, 27

Meesseman, Emma, 8
Most Valuable Player (MVP), 8, 20, 21

National Collegiate Athletic Association (NCAA), 15

Phoenix Mercury, 19

Rookie of the Year, 18

Seattle Storm, 6

University of Connecticut, 12
University of Delaware, 13–14
Ursuline Academy, 12

Washington Mystics, 5–9, 23–24, 27–28
Wilmington, Delaware, 11
WNBA Finals, 5–6, 19, 21, 24–25

**Answer Key: 1.** Answers will vary; **2.** Answers will vary; **3.** B; **4.** C